D1124370

TOTAL
LACROSSE

BY PAUL BOWKER

SportsZone
An Imprint of Abdo Publishing
www.abdopublishing.com

abdopublishing.com

Published by Abdo Publishing, a division of ABDO, PO Box 398166, Minneapolis, Minnesota 55439. Copyright © 2017 by Abdo Consulting Group, Inc. International copyrights reserved in all countries. No part of this book may be reproduced in any form without written permission from the publisher. SportsZone™ is a trademark and logo of Abdo Publishing.

Printed in the United States of America, North Mankato, Minnesota
092016
012017

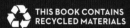

THIS BOOK CONTAINS RECYCLED MATERIALS

Cover Photos: Cecil Copeland/Cal Sport Media/AP Images, foreground; James A. Boardman/Shutterstock Images, background
Interior Photos: James A. Boardman/Shutterstock Images, 1, 40–41; Kevin Rivoli/ Syracuse University/AP Images, 4–5; John Middlebrook/Cal Sport Media/AP Images, 6; Bill Frakes/Sports Illustrated/Getty Images, 8–9; Clifford Skarstedt/Peterborough Examiner/AP Images, 10; George Catlin/Library of Congress, 12–13; North Wind Picture Archives, 14; S&G/Press Association/AP Images, 17; JHU Sheridan Libraries/Gado/ Getty Images, 18–19; Bill Cobb/SuperStock, 21; Bettmann/Getty Images, 22–23; Rich Barnes/Icon Sportswire, 24; CLS Digital Arts/Shutterstock Images, 26–27; Click Images/ Shutterstock Images, 28; Charles Mann/iStockphoto, 31; Svetlana Larina/Shutterstock Images, 32; Mike Broglio/Shutterstock Images, 34–35, 46; Aspen Photo/Shutterstock Images, 36, 44–45; Andy Mead/YCJ/Icon Sportswire/AP Images, 39; Alan C. Heison/ Shutterstock Images, 42; Collegiate Images/Getty Images, 48–49; Geoff Robins/CP/AP Images, 51; Duncan Williams/Cal Sport Media/Newscom, 52–53; Andy Mead/YCJ/Icon Sportswire, 54, 56; Damian Strohmeyer/Sports Illustrated/Getty Images, 58–59; Jonathan Newton/The Washington Post/Getty Images, 61

Editor: Patrick Donnelly
Series Designer: Jake Nordby

Publisher's Cataloging-in-Publication Data

Names: Bowker, Paul D., author.
Title: Total lacrosse / by Paul D. Bowker.
Description: Minneapolis, MN : Abdo Publishing, 2017. | Series: Total sports |
    Includes bibliographical references and index.
Identifiers: LCCN 2016945427 | ISBN 9781680785067 (lib. bdg.) | ISBN
    9781680798340 (ebook)
Subjects: LCSH: Lacrosse--Juvenile literature.
Classification: DDC 796.34--dc23
LC record available at http://lccn.loc.gov/2016945427

CONTENTS

MEN OF LACROSSE

Jim Brown was one of the greatest running backs in college and professional football history. He won the Most Valuable Player (MVP) Award in the National Football League (NFL) four times. But he was a standout in lacrosse, too.

Brown played lacrosse in high school and at Syracuse University in New York. He ended his college career in style. Brown played in the 1957 Collegiate North/South All-Star Game. He scored five goals in one half against the nation's top college players.

Jim Brown was one of the greatest lacrosse players of all time.

Dave Pietramala, *black hat*, gives instructions to his Johns Hopkins Blue Jays.

Brown said the freedom he felt on the lacrosse field was one of his favorite aspects of the game. He thought lacrosse was much less restrictive than football and allowed him to be more creative.

Dave Pietramala was a strong defender. He led Johns Hopkins University to the National Collegiate Athletic Association (NCAA) championship in 1987. He was named the nation's most outstanding defensive player twice. Now he coaches at Johns Hopkins. He was the first person to win NCAA championships in lacrosse as a player and a coach at the same school.

Twin brothers Gary and Paul Gait were among the best to play the game. They introduced the Canadian Box style of play. The "Air Gait" leaping play created by Gary Gait remains famous.

VERSATILE ATHLETES

Jim Brown was not the only football star who took up lacrosse. New England Patriots head coach Bill Belichick played lacrosse in high school and college. Tom Gilburg was a punter for the Baltimore Colts in the 1960s. He also was an All-American in lacrosse at Syracuse. Jim Campbell played lacrosse and football at Navy. He flew more than 100 missions as a fighter pilot in Vietnam.

2

Jen Adams is a legend in women's lacrosse. The Australian distinguished herself at the University of Maryland from 1998 to 2001. She led the Terrapins to four straight national titles. She also was named national player of the year three times. Since 2001 the Tewaaraton Award has been given every year to the top college lacrosse player in the country. Adams was the first to receive the women's award.

Adams scored 445 goals and had 178 assists in her collegiate career. She was the first woman to

Jen Adams in action against Georgetown in 2001

Hannah Nielsen, *right*, battles a US player in the World Women's Under-19 gold medal game in 2007.

reach those totals. She is considered by many to be the best player in women's lacrosse history.

Other female pioneers have helped popularize lacrosse. Kelly Amonte Hiller was the first woman to win nine NCAA titles. She won two as a player at Maryland. She won seven more through 2016 as a coach at Northwestern University.

Hannah Nielsen played for Amonte Hiller at Northwestern. She broke Adams's NCAA career assists record. Nielsen finished her career with 224 assists. She once had 10 assists in a game. She also is a native of Australia. And she won a world championship with the Australian National Team.

Devon Wills won two World Cups with the United States as a goalie. She was named player of the match in the 2009 World Cup title game against Australia. She started all seven US games in the 2013 World Cup.

Taylor Cummings won four high school lacrosse championships. She went on to star at the University of Maryland.

STRONG AND SMART

Katie Schwarzmann was a World Cup medalist for the United States in 2013. She also was a star midfielder at the University of Maryland. Schwarzmann excelled in the classroom, too. She earned all-conference academic honors all four years at Maryland. She graduated in 2013. Two years later she earned a master's degree at Mount St. Mary's University.

3

A PROUD
OLD GAME

Lacrosse is so old that it's nearly impossible to track its exact origin. It dates back to the days before Europeans settled North America.

Lacrosse had no written rules in the early days. The American Indians who first played it had no written language. Players within tribes taught each other. Historians note that some tribes believed the game was a gift from the spirit world. Some tribesmen were buried with their lacrosse sticks. They believed if they took their sticks with them they would be able to play forever.

American Indians play a game similar to lacrosse near Fort Gibson, Oklahoma.

Lacrosse served many purposes to the early American Indian tribes that played it.

The North American tribes played for recreation and to settle disputes between tribes. They also played to toughen young warriors. A lacrosse battle could involve thousands of players. Goals might be placed miles apart. The Iroquois were the first to limit the number of players. They also established clear field boundaries. It was a step closer to the game as it looks today.

French missionaries in the early 1600s were some of the first Europeans to see the game. The missionaries began calling it "lacrosse." That comes from the French word for the crooked stick used in field hockey. Lacrosse sticks and balls were made from natural materials. They usually didn't last long. Balls were made of wood or rocks wrapped in animal skins.

The modern version of lacrosse became popular in Canada in the 1840s. It officially

NOT JUST A GAME

Tribal games of lacrosse sometimes became quite violent. Players were wounded or sometimes even died. Games could last all day. A fight after a match in 1845 between Cherokee teams resulted in dead and injured players. Violence often occurred after a match or in the next few days. After a match in 1790, the losing tribe looked for revenge. Approximately 500 were killed the next day in an attack by Choctaw warriors.

Some early lacrosse balls were much lighter than those used today. They were made of leather and stuffed with hair.

became the national game of Canada in 1867. The game has become popular in many nations. Besides Canada, the United States, Australia, and England are lacrosse hotbeds. So are France, Belgium, Japan, and the Czech Republic.

The game is played by youth and adults. It is played in high school and college. Professional leagues give players a chance to make a living playing the game.

The Canadian lacrosse team celebrates winning the Olympic gold medal in 1908.

4

FAMOUS STADIUMS

Fenway Park in Boston is one of the most famous parks in baseball. It opened in 1912. But the most famous lacrosse stadium is even older.

Homewood Field in Baltimore, Maryland, opened in 1908. The Johns Hopkins University Blue Jays play there. Homewood soon became a hub for men's and women's lacrosse. The Johns Hopkins men's team won five national championships in the 1920s. Two of those teams were unbeaten. They've become one of the most successful programs in NCAA history.

Johns Hopkins does battle with Oxford-Cambridge at Homewood Field in 1926.

Homewood was home to the World Lacrosse Games in 1982. More than 40,000 spectators watched. It featured teams from the United States, Canada, Australia, and Great Britain.

INDOOR PALACES

Indoor lacrosse traces its roots to the 1920s. It is also known as box lacrosse. Box lacrosse was created for indoor stadiums with smaller spaces for players to run. The physical play appealed to spectators. In the 1930s, the American Box Lacrosse League (ABLL) held games in famous stadiums such as Madison Square Garden in New York City.

Homewood Field remains a popular and historic setting for lacrosse. The Carrier Dome in Syracuse, New York, is another. The indoor stadium is famous for hosting football and basketball games. But the Syracuse lacrosse tradition is carried on there as well.

Navy-Marine Corps Memorial Stadium in Annapolis, Maryland, is located on the US Naval Academy campus. A sellout crowd usually packs the stands for the Army–Navy men's lacrosse games.

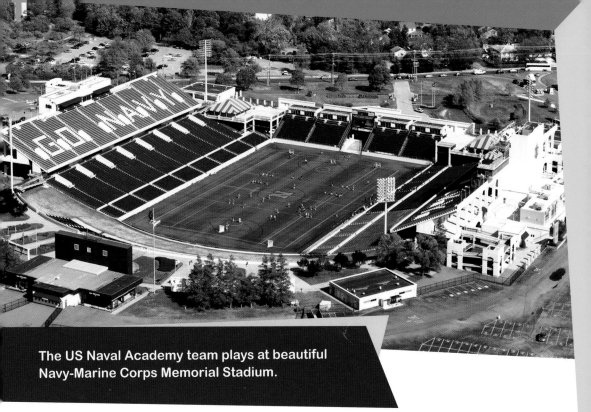

The US Naval Academy team plays at beautiful Navy-Marine Corps Memorial Stadium.

Jackson Field at Wesleyan University in Connecticut is known as "The Birdcage." It's bordered by stately old trees and modern art buildings. On warm days, students often watch the action from inflatable pools on the sideline.

Salisbury University in Maryland is home to Sea Gull Stadium. The original Sea Gull Stadium was a difficult place for visiting teams to play. That all changed in 2016 when a new Sea Gull Stadium opened. The $19 million renovation turned it into one of the nicest stadiums in the country.

5

COACHING LEGENDS

Jim Brown might have been the best lacrosse player in history. Roy Simmons Sr. had a lot to do with Brown's success.

Simmons built a lacrosse powerhouse at Syracuse University. He coached from 1932 to 1970. He also was a longtime assistant coach of the Syracuse football team. Simmons carved the path for a long list of both men's and women's lacrosse coaches. His son and his grandson followed him into coaching. Simmons won 251 games in 38 years. He was inducted into the Lacrosse Hall of Fame in 1964.

Roy Simmons Sr., *left*, discusses football strategy with Syracuse head coach Dick Bell and future NFL star Floyd Little.

Simmons wasn't alone in his love of lacrosse. Dick Garber coached men's lacrosse at the University of Massachusetts from 1955 to 1990. He is known as the father of lacrosse in New England. He was the first NCAA Division I coach to win 300 games.

Kelly Amonte Hiller was a star in women's lacrosse at Maryland. She was part of two national championship teams as a player. Then she became a coaching star at Northwestern University. She led the Wildcats to seven national championships in 10 years. Her 2005 Northwestern team went unbeaten. It was the first women's team outside of the eastern standard time zone to win the national title.

ALL ABOUT SIMMONS

Roy Simmons Sr. played for Syracuse University in the 1920s. He became the school's second lacrosse coach in 1931. He retired in 1970 after 231 wins. Roy Simmons Jr. took over and coached until 1998. His teams won six national championships. Roy Jr.'s son, Roy III, became an assistant coach under his dad. Then he coached under John Desko.

Kelly Amonte Hiller is one of the most successful coaches in the history of women's lacrosse.

6

TOOLS OF THE GAME

The stick is the most vital tool of the game. Its length and size will depend on which position you play. And you need a good one to play well.

Of course, lacrosse players need a lot of other equipment, too. Boys and men need arm guards, gloves, helmets, and a variety of protective padding. Girls and women need protective eyewear. Everybody needs mouthguards, shoes, and a game jersey. Shorts and socks are a must for all players as well.

Finding the right stick is an important part of gearing up for lacrosse.

Shorter sticks are a better fit for young players who are just developing their skills.

Most sporting goods stores carry the equipment. Pick a store that sells a wide selection of lacrosse gear. Some stores rent equipment. That might help a beginner who isn't ready to spend a lot of money on a new sport.

Sticks come in different lengths. Defenders' sticks generally are longer. That helps them with stick checking. These sticks usually range from 42 to 46 inches (107 to 117 cm) long.

Beginners should start out with a shorter stick, because it's easier to handle and catch passes with it. Some sticks may be as short as 34 inches (86 cm). These are usually for players age 12 and under. For older players, the shorter sticks are approximately 40 inches (102 cm). Some players prefer shorter sticks. They can control the ball better than with a longer stick. Shorter sticks are better for the indoor game. Longer sticks are used more in outdoor games.

Many lacrosse sticks are sold with the mesh pocket already strung. This means that they are ready right away. But there are differences between pockets. Some players prefer a soft mesh. Others want a firmer pocket. Players can string two to four shooting laces across the pocket. They provide better control when shooting or passing.

The shafts once were all made of wood. Today they are made of different materials. Beginners will most likely use a stick with an aluminum shaft. More advanced players use shafts made of graphite or titanium.

Lacrosse is a running sport. Shoes should provide support but also allow players to move freely. Basketball sneakers or running shoes provide better ankle support for the indoor game. Outdoor shoes usually have plastic cleats.

STICK MODIFICATIONS

If you're a beginner and can't find a shorter stick, don't worry. You can buy a full-size stick and cut it down to size. But don't do it yourself. The sporting goods store should be able to trim it down correctly. Be sure to check with your league to find out the minimum length required.

Pick a helmet that fits snugly. Most players wear a cage instead of a plastic visor to protect the face. A visor can be uncomfortably hot in warm weather. And it is likely to fog up and block the player's vision. Helmets are not required in girls' lacrosse except for goalkeepers.

Your gloves should be a good fit—not too loose or tight. Lacrosse gloves are lighter and

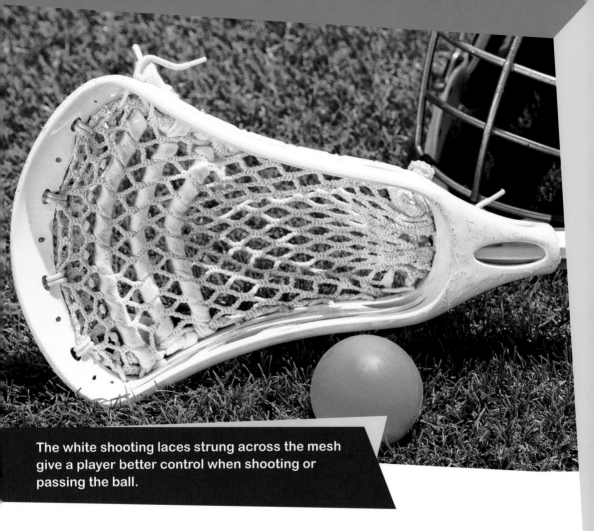

The white shooting laces strung across the mesh give a player better control when shooting or passing the ball.

more flexible than hockey gloves. They allow a player to better control the stick and the ball.

Other important equipment guards the body from bumps and bruises. There are guards or pads to protect wrists, elbows, and arms. Shoulders, ribs, kidneys, and knees need protective gear as well.

Goalkeeping equipment is more extensive. The stick is different. Its head is bigger to stop more shots. Its pocket is deeper to keep the ball from bouncing out. Goalies wear additional protection around the hips, chest, and throat. They also use thicker gloves and shin guards.

Mouthpieces are required in youth lacrosse. They're common among older players, too.

Lacrosse players are protected by a variety of different pads and guards.

33

7

GETTING STARTED

One of the most important plays in lacrosse is the draw. It's also known as a faceoff. The draw is held in the middle of the field at the start of the game. A draw also begins play at the beginning of each period and after a goal is scored.

Possession is key in lacrosse. You need to have the ball to score. The best way to get the ball is to win the draw.

The draw begins with one player from each team in the center circle in boys' or men's lacrosse. The players squat into a low position. Their sticks

Teams that are successful on the draw—or faceoff—usually possess the ball more than their opponents.

are held on the ground in a back-to-back position. Both hands must be on the stick. The players may not make contact with each other before the draw is taken.

The referee places the ball between the two sticks. He or she then blows the whistle to begin play. The center players use a variety of techniques to pick up the ball or deflect it to a teammate.

The draw in the girls' and women's game is a bit different. The players do not hold their sticks to the ground. Instead they hold them horizontally and waist-high with the pockets facing in. The referee places the ball between the two sticks.

CHAMPION'S SECRET

Northwestern University women's lacrosse coach Kelly Amonte Hiller points to her teams' success with the draw as a key factor in their dynasty. The Wildcats won seven national championships in eight years. Eight straight draw wins in the 2012 championship game led to a Northwestern title.

Players who aren't taking the draw line up on the edge of the center circle.

The players push their sticks together to hold the ball in place. A whistle from the referee begins play.

Different techniques are used to win draws. The clamp-and-step style is used often in the boys' and men's game. This is because play begins with the sticks on the ground. But you must be quick. As the whistle sounds, push your right hand down on the stick. Move your left hand upward to your left shin. Clamp the head of your stick over the ball. Use your shoulders and forearm to drive into your opponent. A quick step with your right foot provides positioning for the clamp. Shield your opponent from the ball and pick it up.

In 2016 Syracuse senior Kayla Treanor led the NCAA by controlling 217 draws in 24 games.

Kayla Treanor led the NCAA in draws controlled in 2016.

8

A GAME OF THEIR OWN

In 1926 a girls' high school in Baltimore, Maryland, organized a lacrosse team. Bryn Mawr became the first school in the United States to have a women's lacrosse team. Enthusiasm for the sport soon spread to other East Coast schools. Today girls' lacrosse is one of the fastest-growing sports in the country. More than 138,000 girls played high school lacrosse in 2013. The number of schools with girls' lacrosse had grown by more than 36 percent in a five-year period.

The girls' game differs from the boys' game. The draw is different. Also, body checking is illegal in

Girls' lacrosse is becoming increasingly popular throughout the United States.

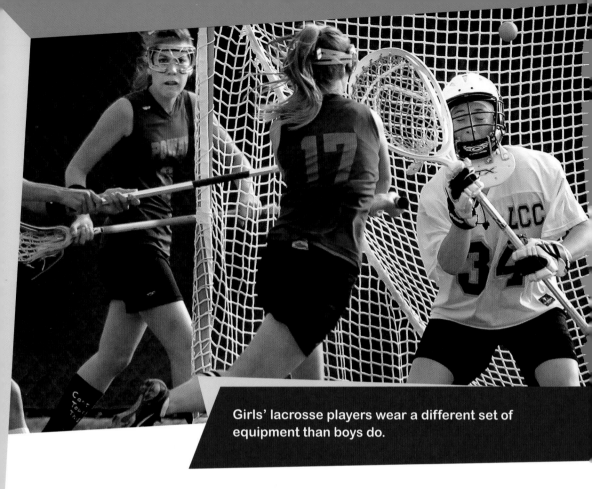

Girls' lacrosse players wear a different set of equipment than boys do.

the girls' and women's game. Stick checking is even forbidden for girls younger than seventh grade. That rule is designed to let the players learn the game and perfect their skills. They can focus on catching and cradling the ball, passing, shooting, and footwork.

There are still times when sticks may hit each other. This is not necessarily a foul. Sometimes one stick may hit another because of the players' positioning. Modified stick checking can be done though. This happens when a player cradling the ball is doing so with her stick below shoulder level. A stick check done above the shoulder is a foul.

Sticks must never come near the head of a player. Players may not move their sticks inside an imaginary 7-inch (18-cm) sphere around each player's head. An attacker may not cradle the ball in her stick and hold it within that sphere.

Lightweight sticks made of aluminum or titanium allow girls to move quickly around and through opponents. That makes the game easier to play.

SIMILAR EQUIPMENT

Girls wear much of the same equipment as the boys. But they don't need as much padding because there's no checking. Footwear for girls includes running shoes or athletic shoes with rubber cleats. All players wear mouthguards and eye protection. Some players wear gloves. Nose protection and soft headgear is allowed. Goalies wear a helmet with a facemask, a throat protector, and a chest protector. Goalies also can wear additional protection for their legs and arms.

9

THE ART OF CRADLING

If your team wins the draw, you might get the ball. But you need to know how to cradle it to keep it.

Cradling involves keeping the ball in the pocket of your stick while you run down the field. It is important to master cradling. As a beginner you usually need to look at the ball while cradling it. After enough practice you won't need to look. You will know the ball is there because of how the stick feels. This will allow you to look at the net or at opposing players while running. You won't have to worry about where the ball is.

A vertical cradle puts you in position to pass or shoot quickly.

The one-handed cradle allows the player with the ball to ward off opponents with his or her free hand.

Cradling is one of the first skills a lacrosse beginner should learn. It's crucial to keeping the ball. The cradle can be done in a side-to-side, up-and-down, or back-and-forth rocking motion.

Players use several different cradling techniques. You can hold your stick horizontally or vertically. You can use one or two hands. Your top hand will do most of the work when using both hands. Your bottom hand will act as more of a guide.

The two-handed horizontal cradle is one of the first cradles to learn. It's especially effective in the open field. In this cradle you rock the ball back and forth as you run. If you're in heavy traffic and need to protect the ball, the vertical cradle works well. You're also ready to pass or shoot quickly with a vertical cradle. A one-handed vertical cradle is used mostly by attackers and midfielders. It helps you protect the stick while fighting off pressure from opponents.

GROUND BALLS

Picking up a ground ball in the open field is another skill that creates possession for your team. Concentrate on this in practice. As you approach the ball, bend at your knees. Lower your stick's head to just above the ground. Pick up the ball in one scooping motion. Establish a good cradle and run.

10

GREAT PLAYS

Gary Gait caused a buzz in 1988. He used an unusual move that became known around the world as the "Air Gait." The move was eventually outlawed by the NCAA. But lacrosse fans still talk about the play.

Gait's Syracuse team faced Pennsylvania in the NCAA semifinals. Gait stood behind the Penn net with the ball. Defenders expected him to pass to a teammate or run in front of the net to take a shot. Instead, Gait ran at the back of the net. He jumped and slammed the ball over the crossbar. It went into the net for a goal. He did it again later in the game.

Gary Gait beats the Penn defense on the "Air Gait" play that made him famous.

Another Syracuse star relied on his power in front of the net to score. Jim Brown reportedly could skip a shot off the turf at 90 miles (144 km) an hour. Not many goalies had quick enough reflexes to stop his shot. And few had the guts to stand in front of it.

How about three goals in the blink of an eye? Drexel men's lacrosse scored three times in 11.3 seconds in a 2014 NCAA Tournament game against Penn. Nick Saputo scored two of the Dragons' goals. Drexel tacked on three more goals in a 64-second span in the second half. The Dragons won the game 16–11. John Grant Jr. amazed crowds during his college and pro career. He surprised defenders with backhanded shots over his shoulder or between his legs. He scored his 636th career

DAVE PIETRAMALA

Dave Pietramala was the first person to win the NCAA Division I national championship as both a player and a coach. He was a standout defensive player at Johns Hopkins University. Then he returned to the school as its men's lacrosse coach. He was known as a takeaway defenseman who dominated the game. He was named the most outstanding defenseman in the nation twice.

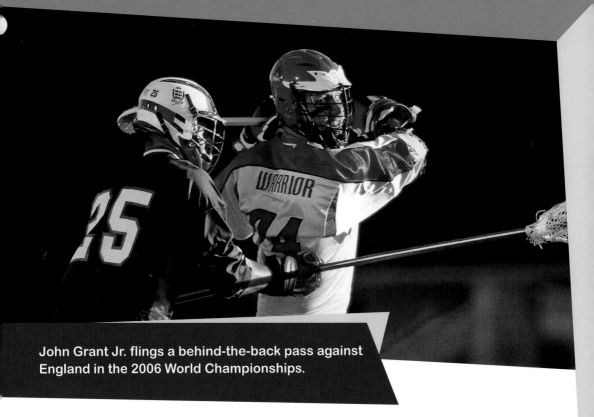

John Grant Jr. flings a behind-the-back pass against England in the 2006 World Championships.

professional goal in 2015. That moved him past Gait into second place in National Lacrosse League history.

Jen Adams displayed her wicked backhand shot in the 1999 NCAA women's championship game. The Maryland star took a pass from a teammate. Then in one sweeping motion, she sent a backhand shot past the Virginia goalie. That was one of four goals Adams scored in that title game.

DEFENDING THE NET

The goalkeeper on any lacrosse team is the last line of defense. Goalies can make a huge difference in a game. The best have proven their importance time and again.

Brian Dougherty helped lead Team USA to a 2010 world title. He had 15 saves in a 12–10 win over Canada in the International Lacrosse Federation (ILF) World Championship final. Two of his biggest saves came in a late flurry in the fourth quarter to keep the Canadians off the scoreboard.

Brian Dougherty, *right*, defends the goal for the Long Island Lizards in 2009.

Devon Wills had a similar performance for the US Women's National Team. It came in the 2009 ILF World Cup championship game. She made seven saves as the United States edged Australia 8–7 for the gold medal.

Goalies have a few advantages that other players on the field don't have. Their sticks have a much larger pocket. They wear the most protective equipment. In girls' lacrosse, the goalkeeper is the only one wearing a helmet. And they are allowed to block or bat the ball away with their hands.

Brian Dougherty was named MVP of the 1995 NCAA Tournament even though his team didn't win the title.

A goalie must wear a helmet, a mouthguard, a face guard, gloves, a throat protector, and a chest protector. The goalie

Goalies use bigger heads on the ends of their sticks. And in girls' and women's lacrosse, they're the only players who wear helmets.

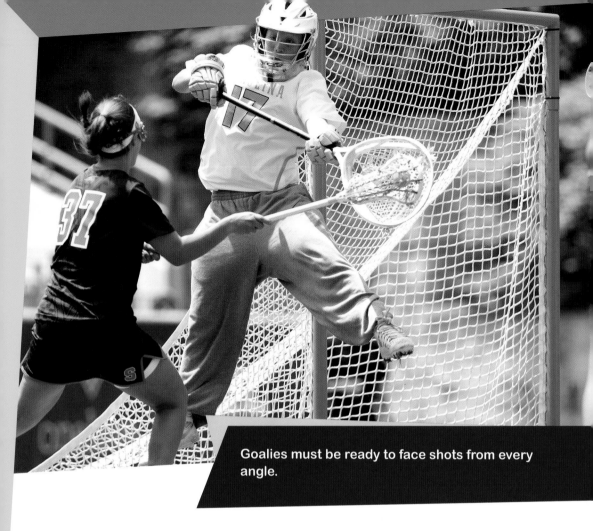

Goalies must be ready to face shots from every angle.

stick is bigger than the sticks used by field players. The pocket is much wider. This helps them make saves.

Goalies are protected by more than just padding. The rules look out for their safety as well. Opposing players can't touch them as long as goalies are in the crease area. The crease is a circle around the net with an 18-foot (5.5-m) diameter.

However, goalkeepers must be careful. They cannot enter the crease with the ball if they get possession of the ball outside the crease. That's a foul. The other team is rewarded possession if the foul is called.

The goal is a square that's 6 feet high and 6 feet wide (1.8 m by 1.8 m). Goalkeepers face a variety of shots. Some fly in high and hard. Others are aimed at the ground. They can be skipping along the turf or coming in on a bounce. To stop them, goalies need to hold their sticks at different angles. Sometimes they hold the stick with the pocket at shoulder or head height. At other times it's best to keep the pocket close to the ground. Quickness and confidence are important. And awareness comes with experience.

TREVOR TIERNEY

Trevor Tierney might be the best role model a goalkeeper could have. He was the first goalkeeper to win an NCAA, professional, and ILF world championship. Tierney won two national titles at Princeton. He led the Baltimore Bayhawks to the 2005 Major League Lacrosse title. Tierney also was named All-World and won a gold medal for Team USA in the 2002 ILF World Championships.

12

GORILLAS OF THE FIELD

They were known as Garber's Gorillas.

Dick Garber was the men's lacrosse coach at the University of Massachusetts (UMass) from 1955 to 1990. His players adopted a winning outlook on their games. Their attitude carried them a long way on the field. Garber was the first NCAA Division I coach to win 300 games. The Minutemen's home field is named after him. He is known as the father of New England lacrosse.

Garber's nickname was "Goose." But he became more closely identified with a different

Brett Garber was the third generation of the Garber family to represent UMass on the lacrosse field.

animal. The gorilla name dates back to the 1960s. It started innocently enough. A player's girlfriend suggested the name. It stuck. Soon students began wearing gorilla suits and masks to UMass lacrosse games. Garber loved it.

BOMBS AWAY!

One of the craziest lacrosse plays ever happened in a 2011 high school game. Matt Borda was a defenseman for Gonzaga College High School in Washington, DC. He was standing behind his net, 80 yards (73 m) from his opponent's goal. He fired the ball down the field. It went over the goalie's head and into the net. A video of the play topped 2 million views on YouTube.

"Coach Garber had gorilla everything. Balls, mugs, hats; you name it," said Greg Cannella, a 1988 UMass graduate.

Cannella is a big part of Garber's legacy in the lacrosse world. First Ted Garber took over at UMass when his father retired in 1990. He left for another coaching opportunity in 1994. That's when Cannella took over the program. His UMass teams won 183 games through 2016.

Ted Garber had a long career coaching prep and professional lacrosse. Ted's son, Brett,

A video of the amazing goal Matt Borda, *16*, scored in 2011 went viral.

became the third generation of Garbers to represent UMass lacrosse. In 2004 he joined the team his grandfather had made famous. He helped the Minutemen reach their first NCAA final four in 2006. Brett Garber went on to star for the Boston Cannons of Major League Lacrosse. He was just the latest Garber to leave his mark on New England lacrosse.

GLOSSARY

alloy
A material made of two or more metals, or of a metal and other material.

assist
A pass that leads to a goal for a teammate.

attacker
Also called a forward, the player usually located in a team's offensive end trying to score goals.

cradle
To hold the ball in the pocket of a lacrosse stick while running.

draw
A faceoff between two opposing players inside the center circle.

ground ball
A loose ball on the ground that players try to scoop up with their sticks to gain possession.

mesh
An interlaced structure often made from cloth or wire threads.

pocket
The end of a lacrosse stick where the ball is carried.

sphere
A three-dimensional circle; in girls' and women's lacrosse, the sphere refers to an area around a player's head that opponents are not allowed to enter or interfere with in any way.

stick check
An attempt by a player to knock the ball away from an opponent by hitting that player's stick.

FOR MORE INFORMATION

Books

Amonte Hiller, Kelly. *Winning Women's Lacrosse*. Champaign, IL: Human Kinetics, 2010.

Bowker, Paul. *Girls' Lacrosse*. Minneapolis, MN: Abdo Publishing, 2014.

Urick, David. *Sports Illustrated Lacrosse: Fundamentals for Winning*. Lanham, MD: Taylor Trade Publishing, 2008.

Websites

To learn more about lacrosse, visit **booklinks.abdopublishing.com**. These links are routinely monitored and updated to provide the most current information available.

INDEX

ABOUT THE AUTHOR

Paul D. Bowker is an editor and author who splits his time between Hyannis, Massachusetts, and Chesterton, Indiana. His 30-year newspaper career has included several years as a lacrosse writer. He is a national past president of Associated Press Sports Editors and has won several national writing awards.